Magnets

Heinemann
LIBRARY

Karen Bryant-Mole

First published in Great Britain by Heinemann Library, Halley Court, Jordan Hill, Oxford OX2 8EJ
a division of Reed Educational & Professional Publishing Ltd.

OXFORD FLORENCE PRAGUE MADRID ATHENS MELBOURNE AUCKLAND KUALA LUMPUR
SINGAPORE TOKYO IBADAN NAIROBI KAMPALA JOHANNESBURG GABORONE PORTSMOUTH
NH (USA) CHICAGO MEXICO CITY SAO PAULO

Designed by Jean Wheeler
Commissioned photography by Zul Mukhida
Consultant – Hazel Grice
Printed in Hong Kong / China

02 01
10 9 8 7 6 5 4 3 2

ISBN 0 431 07838 6

This title is also available in a hardback
library edition (ISBN 0 431 07833 5).

British Library Cataloguing in Publication Data

Bryant-Mole, Karen
  Magnets. - (Science all around me)
  1. Magnets - Juvenile literature
  I. Title
  538.4

A number of questions are posed in this book. They are designed
to consolidate children's understanding by encouraging further
exploration of the science in their everyday lives.

**Words that appear in the text in bold can
be found in the glossary.**

Acknowledgements
The Publishers would like to thank the following for permission to reproduce photographs: Positive Images 6, Zefa 4, 10, 14.

Every effort had been made to contact copyright holders of any material reproduced in this book. Any omissions will be
rectified in subsequent printings if notice is given to the Publisher.

Contents

Magnets   4

Magnetic or non-magnetic?   6

Magnetic force   8

Magnetism through air   10

Magnetism through objects   12

Strength   14

Poles   16

Two magnets   18

Making magnets   20

Permanent magnets   22

Glossary   24

Index   24

Magnets

There is a huge magnet hanging from this crane.

A magnet is a metal that some other metals **cling** to.

Large blocks of squashed-up metal are clinging to this magnet.

(i) *Things that can cling to a magnet are 'magnetic'.*

See for yourself ...

Edward cut out some fish shapes. Then he put a paperclip on each fish and placed them in a pretend pond.

He made a fishing rod from a stick, some string and a magnet. The paperclips on the fish cling to the magnet.

Edward can pull the fish out of the pond.

Magnetic or non-magnetic?

Iron is a magnetic metal. It will **cling** to a magnet. Other metals that have iron in them, such as steel, are magnetic, too.

This boy is putting a metal can into a **recycling** bin. Magnets will be used to sort the cans with iron in them from those without iron.

? *Does your family recycle cans?*

See for yourself ...

Melissa is testing some objects with a magnet.

Magnets that are this shape are called bar magnets.

Things that won't cling to a magnet are 'non-magnetic'. This plastic teaspoon is non-magnetic.

Magnetic force

These keys are **clinging** to two long, thin magnets. They are being pulled in to the magnets by a force called magnetism.

A force is a **scientific** word for a type of push or pull.

When something is pulled in towards a magnet, it is 'attracted' by the magnet.

See for yourself ...

Edward and Alice are playing a travel game.

The board is magnetic. The playing pieces have tiny magnets attached to them.

Edward can feel the magnetic pull when he tries to move a playing piece.

Magnetism through air

Magnets work through air.

This freezer cabinet has a magnetic strip down the side of the door.

When the woman shuts the door, she will feel the magnetism pulling, even when there is still a gap between the freezer and the door.

Can you think of any doors in your home that might have magnetic strips?

See for yourself ...

Bartie is lowering a magnet over some paperclips.

Magnets that are this shape are called horseshoe magnets.

Just before the magnet reaches the paperclips, he sees that they jump up to **cling** to the magnet.

The magnetic force has pulled them up through the air.

Magnetism through objects

Behind each of these little wooden butterflies is a magnet.

The magnets are **clinging** to a magnetic fridge door.

Between the magnet and the door there are pieces of paper.

(i) *Magnetism can work through non-magnetic materials, like paper.*

See for yourself ...

Adam used some fridge magnets and a magnetic **baking tray** to see if the magnet worked through other non-magnetic materials.

He found that the thickness of the material was important.

The magnets worked through thin pieces of plastic, card and **fabric** but not thicker pieces.

13

Strength

Some magnets are stronger than others.

Fridge magnets are quite weak but this magnet is very strong. It can be used to lift lots of metal.

(i) *Magnets pull in magnetic **materials**. The stronger the magnet, the greater its pull.*

See for yourself ...

Alex has two magnets.

She put two paperclips on the edge of a table and slowly pushed one magnet towards one of the paperclips until it started to move.

The second magnet has been pushed in much closer but the second paperclip has still not moved.

The second magnet must be weaker.

Poles

This dressmaker is using a horseshoe magnet to pick up pins. The pins are **clinging** to the two ends.

The ends of a magnet are called its poles.

One end is called the north pole and the other the south pole.

(i) *The poles of a magnet have the strongest pull.*

See for yourself ...

Berta has pushed a bar magnet into a pile of paperclips.

When she lifts the magnet, she can see that most of the paperclips are clinging to the ends of the magnet.

Two magnets

These two magnets are **clinging** to each other.

If one magnet's north pole faces the other magnet's south pole, the two magnets will be attracted to each other.

If the same poles face each other, the magnets are pushed apart.

 This pushing apart is called repelling.

See for yourself ...

Alice's toy train carriages have a magnet on each end.

One magnet has its south pole facing outwards. The other has its north pole facing outwards.

Alice can feel the two magnets repelling when she tries to join the carriages with the same poles facing each other.

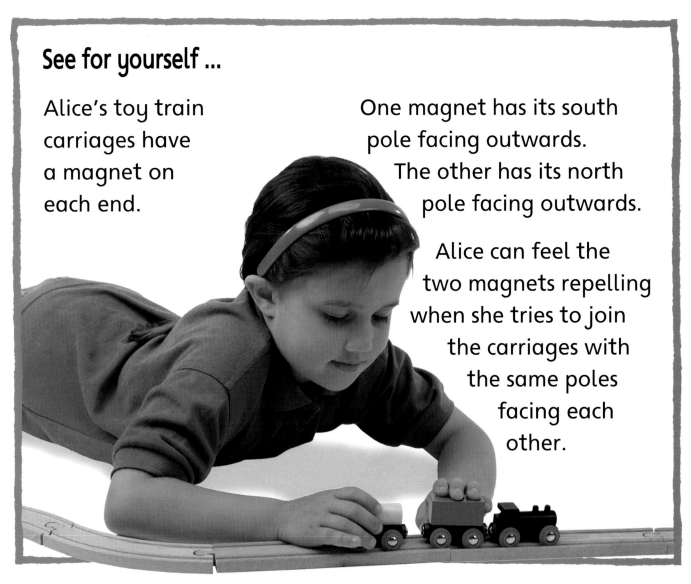

Making magnets

When something that is made from a magnetic **material** touches a magnet, it too becomes a magnet.

Anything that becomes a magnet is 'magnetised'. These paperclips are touching a magnet. They have been magnetised.

(i) *When the paperclips are taken off the magnet they stop being magnets.*

See for yourself ...

Things that are only magnetised for a short time are called temporary magnets.

Adam has made a line of paperclips hang off this magnet.

Each new paperclip becomes magnetised and will attract the next paperclip.

When Adam takes them off the magnet, the paperclips stop being magnets.

Permanent magnets

Anything that is a magnet all the time is called a permanent magnet.

These are all permanent magnets.

Magnets are made up of millions of tiny magnets, all facing the same direction.

If a magnet gets knocked, some of the tiny magnets may get moved and the magnet will lose some of its magnetism.

See for yourself ...

Permanent magnets slowly get weaker as time goes on.

Special pieces of soft iron, called 'keepers', can help to stop this happening.

Melissa is putting a keeper onto this horseshoe magnet.

The more care you take of your magnets, the longer they will last.

Glossary

attached fastened

baking tray a flat, metal tray

cling(-ing) is pulled in and held

fabric cloth

materials what things are made from

recycling using again

scientific to do with science

Index

air 10, 11
attract 8, 18
bar magnets 7
card 13
cranes 4
fabric 13
forces 8
fridges 12, 13, 14
horseshoe magnets 11, 16, 23
iron 6, 23

keepers 23
keys 8
magnetised 20, 21
magnetism 4, 8, 10–11, 12–13, 22
metal 4, 6, 14
non-magnetic 7, 12, 13
north poles 16, 18, 19
paperclips 5, 11, 15, 17, 20, 21
permanent magnets 22–23

plastic 7, 13
poles 16–17, 18, 19
pulls 8, 9, 10, 14, 16
recycling 6
repel 18, 19
south poles 16, 18, 1
steel 6
strong 14
temporary magnets 21, 22
weak 14, 15, 23